It happened to me

Mum and Dad split up

Written by
Elizabeth O'Loughlin

Illustrated by
Kayleigh Adams

First published in the UK in 2005
by PANGOLIN BOOKS
Unit 17, Piccadilly Mill, Lower Street,
Stroud, Gloucestershire, GL5 2HT.

Copyright © 2005 Bookwork Ltd.

A CIP catalogue record for this book is
available from the British Library.

ISBN 1-84493-020-3

Printed in the UK by Goodman Baylis Ltd.

GETTING HELP WHEN YOUR MUM AND DAD SPLIT UP

If your mum and dad are splitting up, you may be feeling sad and confused. It will help if you talk to someone about how you are feeling. You could talk to your gran, like the child in this book does, or to another adult that you trust. Or you can ring ChildLine or the NSPCC. They will not tell anyone about your call unless you want them to or you are in danger.

Childline
(www.childline.org.uk)
If you have a problem, ring ChildLine on 0800 1111 at any time – day or night. Someone there will try to help you find ways to sort things out.

NSPCC
(www.nspcc.org.uk)
The NSPCC has a helpline on 0808 800 5000 which never closes. There is always someone there to talk to if you are unhappy, worried or scared about something in your life. You can also e-mail them on help@nspcc.org.uk

"We used to live together, Mum and Dad and me. Mum and Dad talked a lot and laughed a lot and played with me a lot, and we all did things together. Mum and Dad were happy, and so was I."

"We don't live together any more, and this is how it happened. I think it started long ago, or perhaps it was only yesterday. I'm not sure.

Mum and Dad talked and laughed only a little, and played with me only a little. Then they never talked and never laughed and I played by myself.

"Sometimes I woke up at night because I heard shouts. I went to look once. Mum and Dad were angry and crying. They didn't look like Mum and Dad. And they didn't sound like Mum and Dad. I cried and shouted too."

"They told me crossly to go to bed, and I wondered what I had done that was so bad. Mum and Dad were sad and angry. I was sad and frightened."

"Then, one day, Mum and Dad told me that we weren't going to live together any more. They frightened me. I didn't understand where I was going to live. How could I be in one house and then another?"

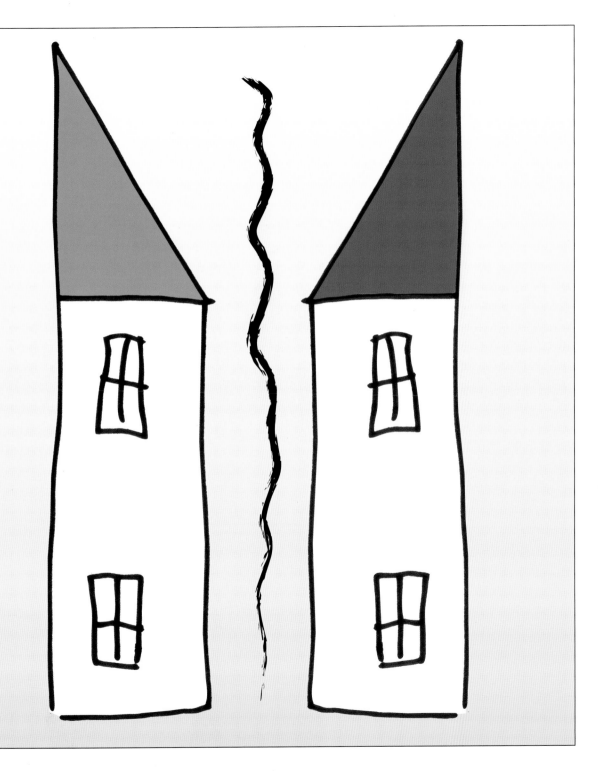

"I didn't understand why I had to live in two houses. I didn't understand why Mum and Dad were so cross with each other.

Then I thought it was because of me, because I had cried and shouted and been more sad than happy. ,,

My gran said it wasn't because of me, and so did other people. Sometimes I believed them and sometimes I didn't.

They told me that one
day I would believe
them all the time.
But I wasn't sure. ”

"I talk to Gran when I'm not sure of something, because Gran knows things and she helps me.

Gran says it's good to talk and not bottle up things inside. This makes me think of a fly I once caught in a bottle, and how it flew around and around and made lots of noise. "

"That's how I feel inside, like a noisy fly that's bottled-up and can't get out. Then I remember Gran. If she's not there, I pretend to talk to her, and then I feel a bit better and not so bottled-up inside."

"At school, my teacher tells me to talk and make up with my friends when we are angry with each other. Perhaps my teacher could tell Mum and Dad to make up and be friends. Then we could all live together again. I will ask Gran."

"Gran says it's different with grown-up people like Mum and Dad, but I don't know why.

Gran says we may never all live together again. She thinks I believe her, but secretly I don't. I think that if I am very good, Mum and Dad will want to live together with me again."

I have two friends who are sad like me. They live sometimes with their mum and sometimes with their dad, but never altogether.

I go and play with my friends, and they come and play with me. Mum and Dad say this is a good idea, and so does Gran. "

"I told my friends about Gran, and how she listens to my bottled-up-inside-me fly. They said they would like someone to talk to too."

Sometimes I don't want to be with anybody. I just want to be on my own. Then I play outside in the garden or with my favourite toys. Sometimes I read a book. Gran says this is a good idea too.

I still often get frightened, and sometimes I feel angry. Then I want to break things. I hope everyone understands how I feel. I think Gran does. "

Gran says that one day I will not be so frightened. I hope she is right. She says she is sure, and she will be sure for me until I can be sure for myself.